THE OF...

D1326611

ANNUAL 2017

Written by Paul Kiddie
Designed by Uta Dohlenburg

A Grange Publication

© 2016. Published by Grange Communications Ltd., Edinburgh, under licence from Rangers Football Club. Printed in the EU.

Photographs © Rangers Football Club.

ISBN: 978-1-911287-13-1

Contents

Back
WHERE WE BELONG

Rangers kissed goodbye to four years in the wilderness when they stormed to Ladbrokes Championship glory. A superb campaign saw them return to their rightful place at the top table of Scottish football and here we take a look back on some of the highlights of another memorable league season at Ibrox.

FRIDAY, AUGUST 7, 2015
Rangers 3, St Mirren 1
Goals: Wallace (2), Shiels

It was just the start the fans had been craving, with Rangers kicking off their Ladbrokes Championship campaign with a confident performance against St Mirren.

A double from Lee Wallace in the first half and a scrambled finish from Dean Shiels a minute from time gave Mark Warburton a win in his first league game in charge.

RANGERS: Foderingham, Tavernier, Wilson, Kiernan, Wallace, Holt (Shiels 60), Halliday, Law, McKay (Templeton 83), Waghorn, Walsh (Clark 60). Subs not used: Kelly, Aird, Hardie, Thompson.

SUNDAY, AUGUST 16, 2015
Alloa Athletic 1, Rangers 5
Goals: Tavernier, Waghorn, Holt, Miller (2)

The outcome of the match at Recreation Park was put beyond doubt by half-time, with Rangers having raced into a 4-1 lead. Although Michael Chopra cancelled out James Tavernier's early strike, normal service was resumed with Martyn Waghorn, Jason Holt and Kenny Miller all on the mark in the opening period. Miller added his second of the match five minutes from time.

RANGERS: Foderingham, Tavernier, Kiernan, Wilson, Wallace, Holt, Halliday, Law (Shiels 61), Miller, Waghorn (Clark 61), McKay (Oduwa 61). Subs not used: Kelly, Ball, Hardie, Walsh.

SUNDAY, AUGUST 30, 2015
Queen of the South 1, Rangers 5
Goals: Halliday, Waghorn (2 pens), Holt, McKay

Rangers surged to another impressive victory when they demolished play-off hopefuls Queen of the South on their own ground.

Martyn Waghorn got a double from the penalty spot and Andy Halliday, Barrie McKay and Jason Holt provided Gers' other goals against a QOS side reduced to 10 men after just two minutes of the second-half when Derek Lyle was red-carded.

RANGERS: Foderingham, Tavernier (Aird 71), Kiernan, Wilson, Wallace (Ball 32), Halliday, Holt, Zelalem, McKay, Miller (Oduwa 66), Waghorn.

Subs not used: Kelly, Law, Shiels, Hardie.

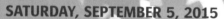

SATURDAY, SEPTEMBER 5, 2015

Rangers 5, Raith Rovers 0

Goals: Wallace, Tavernier, McKay, Waghorn (2)

Another impressive display by Rangers and another five-goal haul, this time with Raith Rovers on the receiving end.

Two up at the break through Lee Wallace and James Tavernier, the hosts added further goals from Barrie McKay and a Martyn Waghorn double.

RANGERS:
Foderingham, Tavernier, Kiernan, Wilson, Wallace, Halliday, Holt (Law 61), Zelalem (Miller 61), McKay, Waghorn, Oduwa (Hardie 70).

Subs not used: Kelly, Thompson, Aird, Ball.

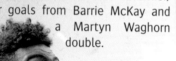

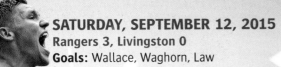

SATURDAY, SEPTEMBER 12, 2015
Rangers 3, Livingston 0
Goals: Wallace, Waghorn, Law

With captain Lee Wallace continuing his goal-scoring habit with the opener against Livingston on the quarter-hour mark, there was never any real doubt about the outcome of the game.

Martyn Waghorn netted four minutes before the break while Nicky Law rounded off another good day at the office with goal no. 3 in the closing stages.

RANGERS:

Foderingham, Tavernier, Kiernan, Wilson, Wallace, Zelalem (Shiels 74), Halliday, Holt (Law 63), McKay (Miller 63), Waghorn, Oduwa. Subs not used: Kelly, Ball, Aird, Hardie.

SUNDAY, SEPTEMBER 27, 2015
Morton 0, Rangers 4
Goals: Waghorn (3), Tavernier

Martyn Waghorn grabbed the headlines with a hat-trick as Rangers romped to an easy victory at Morton.

The striker netted two before the interval and completed his treble tops nine minutes from time. James Tavernier was also on the scoresheet with a first-half effort.

RANGERS: Foderingham, Tavernier, Wilson, Kiernan, Wallace, Halliday, Holt (Miller 62) Zelalem (Shiels 62), McKay (Law 77), Waghorn, Oduwa. Subs not used: Kelly, Ball, Clark, Aird.

SATURDAY, OCTOBER 3, 2015
Rangers 3, Falkirk 1
Goals: Shiels, Tavernier, Wallace

Dean Shiels, James Tavernier and Lee Wallace were the goal heroes for Rangers as they produced a battling performance to beat Falkirk at Ibrox.

Shiels hit a terrific opener before the Bairns replied through Will Vaulks. The score stayed at 1-1 for some time but with nine minutes remaining Tavernier scored another sensational free kick.

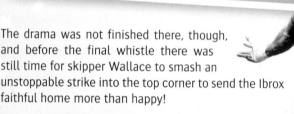

The drama was not finished there, though, and before the final whistle there was still time for skipper Wallace to smash an unstoppable strike into the top corner to send the Ibrox faithful home more than happy!

RANGERS: Foderingham, Tavernier, Kiernan, Wilson, Wallace, Shiels (Ball 90), Halliday, Holt (Law 72), McKay, Waghorn, Oduwa (Miller 61). Subs not used: Kelly, Clark, Hardie, Thompson.

SATURDAY, OCTOBER 17, 2015
Rangers 2, Queen of the South 1
Goals: Holt, Waghorn

In a dramatic finale at Ibrox, Martyn Waghorn missed a late penalty but quickly atoned for his blunder by netting a 90th-minute winner to overcome a battling QOS side.

The visitors from Dumfries had earlier taken the lead in the opening period through Derek Lyle, with Jason Holt cancelling that out eight minutes after the break.

RANGERS: Foderingham, Tavernier, Kiernan, Ball, Wallace, Holt, Halliday, Shiels (Law 57), Miller (Oduwa 57), Waghorn, McKay (Clark 75). Subs not used: Kelly, Aird, Hardie, Thompson.

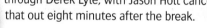

SUNDAY, OCTOBER 25, 2015
St Mirren 0, Rangers 1
Goal: Holt

Midfielder Jason Holt again underlined his value to the team with the only goal of the game to clinch a crucial win which kept Rangers eight points ahead at the top of the table.

His goal with 25 minutes on the clock saw the Light Blues stretch their winning run in the Championship to 11 games.

RANGERS:
Foderingham, Tavernier, Ball, Kiernan, Wallace, Halliday, Zelalem (Shiels 60), Holt, Miller (Clark 60), Waghorn, McKay (Aird 81). Subs not used: Kelly, Thompson, Walsh, Hardie.

TUESDAY, DECEMBER 1, 2015
Rangers 4, Dumbarton 0
Goals: Holt, Waghorn, Oduwa, Halliday

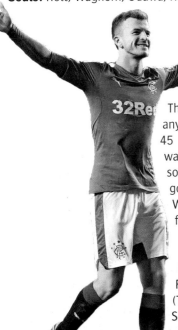

Rangers finally clicked into gear to dispose of Dumbarton at Ibrox Stadium.

The hosts laboured to create any kind of openings in the first 45 minutes but the second half was a different story. We saw some superb football producing goals from Jason Holt, Martyn Waghorn, Nathan Oduwa – his first senior strike – and Andy Halliday.

RANGERS:
Foderingham, Tavernier, Ball, Kiernan, Wallace, Halliday, Holt, Zelalem (Thompson 62), Waghorn (Oduwa 76), Clark, McKay (Miller 62). Subs not used: Kelly, Aird, Hardie, McCrorie.

MONDAY, DECEMBER 28, 2015
Rangers 4, Hibs 2
Goals: Holt (2), Clark, Waghorn

The eagerly anticipated clash didn't disappoint, with 10-man Rangers winning a six-goal thriller to carve open a three-point gap at the top of the table.

Jason Cummings silenced the home support with the opener but Jason Holt blasted a double before the break to send Rangers in at half-time 2-1 ahead. Nicky Clark netted a third and although Dominique Malonga brought Hibs back into things four minutes from time, Martyn Waghorn made the game safe as the whistle approached.

It was a tremendous result for the Light Blues, who had to play the last 20 minutes without the services of Andy Halliday after his dismissal following a clash with Fraser Fyvie.

RANGERS: Foderingham, Tavernier, Kiernan, Wilson, Wallace, Halliday, Law (Clark 62), Holt, Waghorn, Miller (Shiels 62), McKay (Ball 74). Subs not used: Kelly, Zelalem, Oduwa, Thompson.

SATURDAY, JANUARY 2, 2016
Dumbarton 0, Rangers 6
Goals: Miller (3), Waghorn, Halliday, Tavernier

Mark Warburton's side welcomed in the New Year in scintillating fashion as they romped to their biggest win of the season in Durnbarton.

The highlight of the goalfest was a hat-trick for Kenny Miller, with Martyn Waghorn, Andy Halliday and James Tavernier also getting in on the scoring act. Remarkably, all but one of the goals came in the second half.

RANGERS: Foderingham, Tavernier, Wilson, Kiernan, Wallace, Halliday, Holt (Shiels 69), Law (Zelalem 71), Waghorn, McKay, Miler (Clark 69). Subs not used: Kelly, Aird, Oduwa, Thompson.

SATURDAY, JANUARY 16, 2016
Rangers 4, Livingston 1
Goals: Wilson, Waghorn (2), Miller

A superb first-half performance had the points in the bag for the home side as Rangers swept aside the challenge of Livingston in some style.

Danny Wilson set the ball rolling with eight minutes on the clock, before Martyn Waghorn's brace and a Kenny Miller goal had the Light Blues on easy street by half-time.

RANGERS:
Foderingham, Tavernier, Wallace, Wilson, Kiernan, Holt (Shiels 75), Halliday, Law (Zelalem 67), McKay, Miller, Waghorn (Clark 67). Subs not used: Bell, Ball, Thompson, Forrester.

MONDAY, JANUARY 25, 2016
Morton 0, Rangers 2
Goals: Miller, McKay

Rangers rolled their sleeves up to grind out an important victory over their hosts.
Kenny Miller and Barrie McKay netted in either half to take the spoils, though the visitors had to negotiate the final 18 minutes with 10 men after Andy Halliday's red card.

RANGERS: Foderingham, Tavernier, Wallace, Wilson, Kiernan, Zelalem (Forrester 58), Halliday, Law (Shiels 58), McKay, Miller, Waghorn. Subs not used: Bell, Thompson, Hardie, Clark.

SATURDAY, JANUARY 30, 2016
Rangers 1, Falkirk 0
Goal: King

New signing Billy King enjoyed a dream debut for Rangers by netting a stoppage-time winner.
The winger arrived on loan from Hearts two days previously and immediately endeared himself to the supporters with his dramatic contribution as both teams looked set to take a point apiece from the game.

RANGERS: Foderingham, Tavernier, Kiernan, Wilson, Wallace, Law (Forrester 61), Ball, Shiels (Zelalem 77), Waghorn, Miller (King 60), McKay. Subs not used: Bell, Clark, Forrester, Hardie, Burt.

TUESDAY, FEBRUARY 2, 2016
Raith Rovers 0, Rangers 1
Goal: Halliday

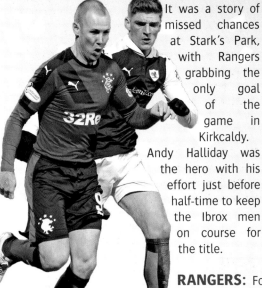

It was a story of missed chances at Stark's Park, with Rangers grabbing the only goal of the game in Kirkcaldy. Andy Halliday was the hero with his effort just before half-time to keep the Ibrox men on course for the title.

RANGERS: Foderingham, Tavernier, Kiernan, Wallace, Ball, Zelalem (Shiels 72), Miller (O'Halloran 64), Halliday, McKay (Forrester 64), Wilson, Waghorn. Subs not used: Bell, Law, Clark, King.

SUNDAY, FEBRUARY 21, 2016
Queen of the South 0, Rangers 1
Goal: Miller

The Light Blues were forced to fight all the way for their victory in Dumfries.

In a tight encounter at Palmerston Park, it took a wonderful effort from Kenny Miller in the second half to bring all three points back to Ibrox.

RANGERS:
Foderingham, Tavernier, Wilson, Kiernan, Wallace, Halliday, Holt, McKay, King (Shiels 60), Clark (Miller 60), O'Halloran. Subs not used: Bell, Law, Ball, Zelalem, Forrester.

SATURDAY, FEBRUARY 27, 2016
Rangers 1, St Mirren 0
Goal: Forrester

Supersub Harry Forrester stepped off the bench to smash his first goal for Rangers and claim a vital three points.

The match looked destined to end in stalemate until his dramatic intervention, his superb curling effort three minutes from time giving Jamie Langfield in the Buddies' goal no chance.

RANGERS:
Foderingham, Tavernier, Kiernan, Wilson, Wallace, Holt (Forrester 70), Halliday, Law (Shiels 60), O'Halliday, Miller, McKay (King 60). Subs not used: Bell, Ball, Clark, Burt.

TUESDAY, MARCH 1, 2016
Rangers 2, Raith Rovers 0
Goals: Forrester, Wallace

A goal in each half was enough to give Rangers a comfortable win over Raith Rovers.

Harry Forrester struck as the half-hour mark approached and captain Lee Wallace doubled his side's advantage shortly

after the break as the Ibrox side took another big step towards the title.

RANGERS:
Foderingham, Tavernier, Kiernan, Wilson, Wallace, Halliday (Ball 81), Holt (Burt 81), Forrester (Shiels 60), O'Halloran, Clark, King. Subs not used: Bell, Miller, McKay, Law.

FRIDAY, MARCH 11, 2016
Rangers 3, Morton 1
Goals: Miller (2), Wallace

Rangers moved 15 points clear at the top of the Championship table after recovering from the shock of going a goal down to record an excellent victory over Morton at Ibrox. Jim Duffy's men took the lead against the run of play on 22 minutes when Denny Johnstone netted. Kenny Miller, though, was in top form and his excellent goals in the 43rd and 48th minutes put Rangers in the driving seat. Lee Wallace capped another magnificent display with his side's third goal of the contest.

RANGERS: Foderingham, Tavernier, Wilson, Ball, Wallace, Holt, Halliday, Forrester (Shiels 46), O'Halloran (King 66), Miller (Clark 77), McKay. Subs not used: Bell, Law, Burt, Thomson.

TUESDAY, APRIL 5, 2016
Rangers 1, Dumbarton 0
Goal: Tavernier

It was party time at Ibrox as Rangers were promoted to the Scottish Premiership after defeating Dumbarton in a nervy affair at Ibrox Stadium.

Four years in the wilderness were ended by James Tavernier's goal early in the second half to spark scenes of celebrations for the club's ever-loyal supporters.

RANGERS: Foderingham, Tavernier, Kiernan, Wilson, Wallace, Halliday, Holt, Forrester (Shiels 78), King, Miller, McKay (O'Halloran 62). Subs not used: Bell, Ball, Law, Zelalem, Clark.

CHAMPIONS
2015-16

I'LL STAY HERE FOR LIFE

Captain Lee happy to finish his career at Ibrox

Captain Incredible Lee Wallace gave the Rangers fans a major boost when he told them he would like nothing better than to finish his career at Ibrox.

The defender arrived in Govan from Hearts in the summer of 2011 and has been one of the Light Blues' outstanding performers since signing his original deal.

His consistency at the back has brought rave reviews and after being an ever-present last season he was voted the PFA Scotland Championship Player of the Year.

Appointed skipper by Mark Warburton, he led by example as Rangers returned to the Premiership in style.

A new contract soon followed, the 29-year-old signing an agreement which commits him to Ibrox until 2019.

LEE LIVES AND BREATHES FOOTBALL.

If Edinburgh-born Lee has his way, however, he'll be staying around for a while longer, following the example of David Weir who played for the club beyond his 40th birthday.

"I would happily finish my career here, that's something I've thought about a lot," said the stopper who has chalked up over 200 games for Rangers.

"If I am performing and doing well enough that the manager deems me good enough to stay, then great.

"And you don't need to look any further than David Weir and how he prolonged his career from being a top professional."

While playing remains his focus for the foreseeable future, the full-back has been taking his first steps on the coaching ladder with the ultimate ambition to move into management when the time is right.

East of Scotland side Tynecastle FC has been benefiting from his experience recently, with the former Hearts star devoting much of his spare time – often at the expense of his young family – to coaching the first team, which he hopes one day will find a route into the SPFL.

"I see big things happening in the future for Tynecastle," said Wallace. "I think about football 24-7 and I want to make progress both for Rangers on the pitch and with my involvement at Tynecastle.

"Tynecastle train twice a week and I'm there for every session I can. I also get to games whenever I can. The guys in the dressing room here at Rangers, mainly Kenny Miller, say they don't know how I get away with spending so much time on football.

"I've got two young kids as well but my wife is well aware it's a big part of my life and she's great about it." He added: "The next step will hopefully be the Lowland League, where you don't have to look any further than Edinburgh City and what they have achieved in getting into the SPFL via the pyramid system.

"I was lucky enough to start coaching with Heriot Vale amateurs, which was run by a lot of my friends. It's a different ball game with Tynecastle which is part-time level in the East of Scotland League. We are hoping to progress the club forward.

"It's quite 24-7. Rangers comes first, I always have to make that clear and it goes without saying – making sure I'm the best I can be for Rangers. But being able to learn a different side of things with Tynecastle has benefited me, made me think differently about the game and helped me all round."

> ❝ I SEE BIG THINGS HAPPENING IN THE FUTURE FOR TYNECASTLE. ❞

JASON HOLT

MUSIC TO HIS EARS

Jason Holt is delighted to have the Rangers fans on his side rather than on his back!

As an opposition player, the former Hearts midfielder felt the full wrath of the Ibrox faithful.

Having swapped Gorgie for Govan, though, he's delighted to hear the supporters sing his praises rather than howl abuse in his direction.

"Moving to Rangers was a fresh challenge for me; a new chapter in my career," said the playmaker.

MIDFIELDER JASON HOLT RELISHING HAVING IBROX FANS ON HIS SIDE.

"Starting that challenge at such a great club as a Rangers player was a fantastic opportunity for me.

"I suppose it was a gamble for both parties but I think it has worked out well for everyone.

"When I have been to Ibrox in the opposition team, it was always such a daunting place to go. But when you're actually playing for Rangers and you have that crowd behind you, it spurs you on so much.

"To have the fans on my side is great and there is no doubt they push the players on.

"Their backing is special and to be able to give a bit back to them by winning the league was great for the players.

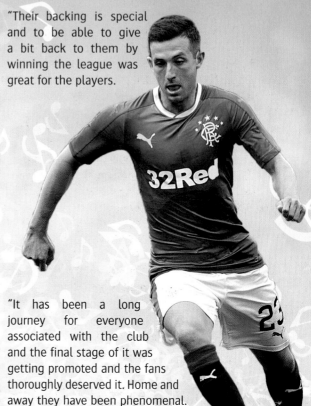

"It has been a long journey for everyone associated with the club and the final stage of it was getting promoted and the fans thoroughly deserved it. Home and away they have been phenomenal. Hopefully we can give them more special times in the future."

Despite assisting Hearts to the Championship the previous season, Rangers' promotion to the Premiership was a career highlight for the 23-year-old.

"Winning the Championship was the aim at the start of that season and to achieve it in such style was tremendous," he said.

"I was proud to play my part in helping the club back to where it belongs in the top flight of Scottish football.

"Unfurling the flag on the opening day of the season was pretty special. It meant so much to the fans and it was special to be part of it.

"I played a small part in Hearts' Championship win but to be heavily involved in Rangers' victory makes it that much better. It was the most I had played in a season and it meant a lot to me to play such a big part in the success.

"Getting the club back was so important for the players, staff and supporters, who have been with us throughout the journey. We wanted to do it for them and it was a brilliant feeling.

"Walking out at Ibrox when we played Dumbarton and needed to win to seal the league was special

and the scenes afterwards made it all the more memorable."

He added: "For a club like Rangers, we only want to be at the top. If we keep working extremely hard, then hopefully we can bring European football back to Ibrox and achieve more cup successes."

Jason quickly established himself as a key player in Mark Warburton's side after impressing on trial and a new contract securing him until 2020 shows the faith the club has in the midfield maestro.

Given his role models in the game, however, his rise to prominence should come as no surprise.

"Growing up, I looked up to a few players in a similar position to me," he explained.

"Andres Iniesta was one I really admired. He doesn't have a massive physique but his ability on the ball was incredible. I tried to study his game and pick up as much as I could.

"In terms of general play, Steven Gerrard and Frank Lampard were the box-to-box midfielders I looked up to. Their knack for scoring goals and being in the right place at the right time was incredible and they had a real talent for making forward runs to impact on games.

" THE MOST IMPORTANT THING IS YOUR QUALITY AS A FOOTBALLER. "

"When they were playing, I would really to try to focus on them as opposed to what was happening elsewhere and try to see what they were doing; how they would read the game and go about their business in matches.

"The most important thing is your quality as a footballer. If you're good enough, you're big enough and I just want to keep improving."

With the likes of Joey Barton and Niko Kranjcar on board for the next stage of the journey, that should be a given.

"Working under the manager and David Weir last season taught me so much and then to have players like Joey Barton, Niko Kranjcar and Jordan Rossiter here can only help the team and enhance all of us," said Jason.

"I am looking to learn as much as I can and I'm sure I will.

"The first thing I noticed about Joey and Niko was what nice people they are. They are very approachable and always looking to help. They have both played at the highest level and bring invaluable experience.

"Jordan's younger than me but his background at Liverpool will also be great for me to learn from. He learned a lot playing there and if I can pick up anything from him I will do."

NIKO KRANJCAR
HUNGRY FOR SUCCESS

"It's a great city for young and ambitious people who want to succeed in life.

"My thought process after Kiev when I didn't play a game for six months was to join a team in pre-season and I got the invitation from Cosmos.

MIDFIELDER NIKO KRANJCAR HAS NO REGRETS AFTER SWAPPING NEW YORK FOR GLASGOW

"I managed to get a space in their team which was great. People could see I was healthy and still able to run about and kick a ball! My main aim was to regain my fitness levels and to play football again after a season that wasn't so great in Kiev.

"All in all, it was a good decision that I needed to make at the time to get back into focus.

"There was an offer on the table from Cosmos but once Rangers came in I really wanted to join.

"I am blessed and happy to get this opportunity. Like everything in life, things could have worked out better or worse so I am just cherishing this moment and where I am at."

Niko Kranjcar enjoyed his bite of the Big Apple – but is now hungry for success in Glasgow.

The Croatian turned down the chance to extend his brief stay with New York Cosmos to pursue his career in the Scottish Premiership with Rangers.

The gifted midfielder had moved to the North American Soccer League – the tier below MLS – in March after an ill-fated spell with Dynamo Kiev.

While he relished life in Manhattan and the unique buzz of the city that never sleeps, the chance to join one of the world's most famous clubs proved irresistible.

The Cosmos wanted him to stay for their 'fall season' but once he became aware of the interest from Ibrox, it didn't take long for the former Tottenham Hotspur and Portsmouth star to accept a new challenge on the other side of the Atlantic.

"New York was interesting! I was in Manhattan and it was very busy and fast! It's a great city, especially for younger people as there are loads of opportunities to find yourself," he said.

"That would make me really happy. I understand and see this as a group project and not about individuals. No-one is bigger than the team and I hope to be a small part of the team which achieves those goals.

"I would definitely like to finish my career at Rangers. It is a great place to be and a great football club.

" EVERYONE IN FOOTBALL KNOWS THE MAGNITUDE OF RANGERS FC. "

The Croat has penned a deal with the Light Blues until the summer of 2018.

If things work out, Niko could see himself finishing his career in Govan.

He said: "Everyone in football knows the magnitude of Rangers FC. I want to win everything there is to win and get into the Champions League. That is what Glasgow Rangers is all about.

"The city is special as well. Glasgow is a big change from New York City but I love it. I am really happy here and delighted to be part of this great experience and football club.

"The people of Glasgow have made a big impression on me, they are so open and friendly.

"The history of the architecture is great and you don't really get that in New York. You can feel the soul of the city on every corner here.

"There are loads of beautiful places and many buildings which add a lot of historical value to the city and I feel quite at home."

PLAYER PROFILES

WES FODERINGHAM

RANGERS secured the signing of goalkeeper Wes Foderingham on a three-year deal with an option for a fourth year in July 2015, the keeper being an ever-present in his first year at the club as Rangers secured the Championship in style.

The six-foot-one shot stopper left Swindon Town after his contract expired and Gers batted away interest from a number of English clubs to steal the 24-year-old's signature. Wes spent four years at the County Ground, making over 150 appearances for The Robins and impressed as the team were promoted by winning League Two in his first season.

He started his career at Fulham before signing his first professional contract with Crystal Palace in August 2010.

He was loaned out to a number of lower league clubs to gain experience before moving to Swindon and never returning to Palace such as was his impact with Town.

MATT GILKS

The keeper signed a two-year deal in the summer following his departure from English Premier League side Burnley.

The Scotland international is vastly experienced having played for a wide variety of clubs in his career.

He began his career at Rochdale in League Two and spent eight seasons there, playing 197 times before being transferred firstly to Norwich City where he made no appearances and then Blackpool in 2008.

Under the management of Ian Holloway, he established himself as the club's first choice stopper and helped them win promotion to the Premier League in 2010.

He played 18 times in England's top flight, in Blackpool's only season there, before they were relegated and Gilks retained his place as top man in the Championship once more. Whilst at Blackpool, he was a regular in the Scotland squad and would have worked closely with Gers goalkeeping coach Jim Stewart – earning three caps for his country.

LEE WALLACE

Lee Wallace has proved himself as Mr Dependable since joining from Hearts in July 2011 for a fee of £1.5 million.

He managed his first Old Firm goal with a fabulous finish in Rangers' sensational 3-2 victory over Celtic in March 2012.

He was then the first high profile star to commit his future to the Light Blues following the administration episode. He was promoted to vice-captain as Rangers began life in the Third Division, and showed his true quality by creating a trademark of charging runs from left-back.

Now captain, he leads by example every week.

Consistent and strong, Lee made his first full international appearance against Japan in October 2009, having previously represented Scotland at U19, U20 and U21 levels.

DANNY WILSON

DANNY WILSON rejoined Rangers in the summer of 2015 on a three-year-deal, five years after departing Ibrox for Liverpool.

The defender returned to the Light Blues after two-and-a-half seasons with Hearts.

He captained the Edinburgh club to the Championship title in 2014/15. In his first spell with Rangers, Wilson made his debut as a 17-year-old.

He left Ibrox having played his part in securing both the league title and the League Cup. Wilson also collected a Scottish Cup medal the previous season after spending the 1-0 win over Falkirk among the unused subs. His international career involves caps for Scotland from under-17 level right through to the full national side.

ROB KIERNAN

RANGERS' manager Mark Warburton was reunited with Kiernan after the defender signed from Wigan on a two-year deal in June 2015.

The pair worked together at Watford where Mark coached a youth side that included Kiernan at the Milk Cup in Northern Ireland.

They were then reunited when Warburton was Sporting Director at Brentford and brought the player on loan from Wigan.

A Republic of Ireland captain at under-19 and under-21 level, Kiernan moved to Glasgow after a loan spell at Birmingham. He had previous experience in Scotland when he spent a short spell on loan at Kilmarnock.

JAMES TAVERNIER

RANGERS signed James Tavernier on a three-year-deal from English League One club Wigan in July 2015 and such was his impact at Ibrox that he signed a 12-month contract extension in the summer.

Born in Bradford, he started his career with Leeds United as an academy player and he spent seven years at Elland Road before he joined Newcastle United in 2008.

He signed pro with the Premier League club in 2009 and despite being a Magpies player until 2014, he only ever made two appearances for the first-team.

Newcastle chose to loan him out to six clubs during his time on Tyneside – Gateshead, Carlisle, Sheffield Wednesday, Milton Keynes Dons, Shrewsbury Town and Rotherham United.

At Rotherham he enjoyed his first major success as a senior player, making 27 appearances, scoring five goals and helping them to promotion to the Championship via the play-offs in the 2013/14 season.

CLINT HILL

The much-travelled defender penned a one-year deal in the summer, his arrival adding experience to the Light Blues' squad having enjoyed a senior career spanning almost two decades in English football.

The left-sided centre-half from Merseyside started his career at Tranmere Rovers and made his first-team debut in the 1997/98 season. He went on to make 140 appearances in five years with the Prenton Park club – playing in the League Cup Final defeat to Leicester City in 2000 – before moving to Oldham Athletic in December 2002 and then Stoke City in the summer of 2003.

In January 2008 the lifelong Liverpool fan joined Neil Warnock's Crystal Palace. Two-and-a-half years later Hill reunited with Warnock at Championship side Queens Park Rangers. QPR suffered the disappointment of being relegated in April 2013 but, with Hill wearing the captain's armband, they won the Championship Playoff Final at Wembley 1-0 against Derby County and were back in England's top flight.

LEE HODSON

The Northern Ireland international put pen to paper on a three-year deal after returning from his country's European Championship campaign in France, his summer arrival bringing added competition at full-back.

The former Watford, Brentford and MK Dons defender spent the second half of last season on loan with Kilmarnock. He made 17 appearances in total for Killie including two against the Light Blues.

Having been part of Northern Ireland's squad in France, Hodson enjoyed a short break before joining up with Mark Warburton's squad on its return from South Carolina and the pre-season training camp.

JASON HOLT

Rangers are set to enjoy the best of Jason Holt, with the midfielder contracted to the club until 2020. Rangers' fans will remember the diminutive midfielder for his impressive strike against Gers in Hearts' 2-0 victory at Tynecastle in November 2014. That was one of two goals he netted for Hearts during the 2014/15 campaign before he moved to Sheffield United in January 2015 for the remainder of the season.

Holt made 11 starts for the League One side and scored five goals. That wasn't his first loan away from Tynecastle, Holt also had a spell with Raith Rovers during the 2011/12 season – he made five appearances for the Fife side and scored once in his time at Stark's Park.

Born and bred in Edinburgh, Holt had been at Hearts since he was nine having risen through their youth system to progress to the first team. He played his boys football for Musselburgh Windsor before joining Hearts in 2002.

He went on to turn out for the Capital side 62 times and scored seven goals, two of those coming against Celtic.

NIKO KRANJCAR

With a top-level career spanning 15 years, the vastly experienced Croatian has been another valuable addition to the squad.

Born in Zagreb, he started his senior professional career at Dinamo Zagreb, becoming the club's youngest captain at 17. Portsmouth gave him his first taste of English football at 22, with Harry Redknapp paying €5 million in August 2006 for one of football's rising stars.

Prior to this switch the young Croat was handed an international debut against Israel by his father Zlatko and he would go on to make 81 appearances for his country, scoring 16 goals. In nine years – from 2004 to 2013 – he would represent Croatia at the 2006 World Cup and at Euro 2008 and Euro 2012.

The 2008 FA Cup winner with Portsmouth became the third Croatian to play for Rangers – following in the footsteps of Dado Prso and Nikica Jelavic.

BARRIE McKAY

The winger made his Rangers debut against St Johnstone in the Light Blues' last game of the 2011/12 season. Having been released by Kilmarnock in August of 2011, his first outing marked a massive turnaround in his fledgling career. He was promoted to the first team ahead of the 2012/13 season and struck Gers first-ever league goal outside the top flight.

His pace and trickery often see him playing out wide, but he has also shown himself to be effective playing off a main striker.

McKay agreed a new five-year contract in September of 2012. He was loaned out for the second half of the 2013/14 season to Morton, where he scored three goals in 14 starts. At the start of the 2014/15 he was sent out on loan again, this time to Championship Raith Rovers. The arrival of Mark Warburton marked a resurgence in his career as he became an integral part of the new manager's plans. He won PFA Goal of the Season 2015-16, was voted Rangers' Young Player of the Year and was called up to the Scotland squad.

KENNY MILLER

The evergreen striker is enjoying his third spell at the club and is as potent as ever in front of goal. He became one of only five post-war players to play for both Old Firm clubs when he signed for Celtic in 2006. He spent only a season at Parkhead before signing for Derby County for a year.

Kenny returned north of the border for a hugely successful period between 2008 and 2011. He won three top-flight league titles, the Scottish Cup and the League Cup during Walter Smith's reign.

The front man made his Scotland debut in 2001, in a friendly against Poland and he scored his first international goal against Iceland in March 2003. The striker went on to make 68 appearances for his country, netting 18 goals.

MICHAEL O'HALLORAN

The attacker pledged his commitment to Rangers by leaving St Johnstone and agreeing a deal until 2020.

He began his senior career at Bolton Wanderers and had spells on loan at Sheffield United, Carlisle United and Tranmere Rovers before moving to Perth in January 2014. There, he made a total of 89 appearances and scored 16 goals. He also has six European appearances under his belt from St Johnstone's recent travels on the Continent and started their Scottish Cup Final win over Dundee United in 2014.

JORDAN ROSSITER

Highly-rated midfielder Jordan Rossiter signed a four-year-deal at Ibrox in May 2016 to leave Liverpool, the club he had been at since a boy.

The England youth had been courted by a number of top clubs before electing to join the Gers after being sold on the club by head of recruitment Frank McParland and the Rangers management team.

Rossiter made five first team appearances for his boyhood club after captaining and graduating from the Liverpool academy, including featuring against Sion in the Europa League, Jurgen Klopp's first game in charge of the Merseyside club.

He also scored his only goal for the Reds to open the scoring in stunning style against Middlesbrough, in a League Cup tie which saw the Reds win 14-13 on penalties.

MARTYN WAGHORN

The striker netted his first Rangers goal on his competitive debut against Hibs in July 2015 and doubled his tally that afternoon, too. 'Waggy' scored the first hat-trick of his career against Morton on September 27 2015, going on to be crowned the club's top scorer last season with 28 goals to his credit.

Born in South Shields, he began his career not too far away in Sunderland, where he made eight appearances before being loaned out to Charlton Athletic and Leicester City. As a 17-year-old, Martyn made his Sunderland debut on Boxing Day 2007 against Manchester United. His first senior goal arrived when on loan at the Valley for Charlton in December 2008 as he struck in a 2-2 draw with Derby County.

The striker has international honours at youth level, representing England's under-19s twice and also the under-21s twice. In his two appearances at under-21 level against Azerbaijan and Israel, he scored in both matches.

He wears the No. 33 shirt due to superstitions about the number.

JOSH WINDASS

The son of former Aberdeen striker Dean Windass, Josh was secured on a pre-contract in January 2016 alongside his Accrington Stanley team-mate Matt Crooks.

The pair signed agreements in the New Year which saw them join up with Mark Warburton's side in the summer.

The pacey midfielder began his career at Huddersfield Town before a leg break forced him to give up the game for a short period, working as a labourer. He began playing non-league football for Harrogate Railway Athletic before Accrington Stanley made a move for him.

Windass spent three years at Stanley making 75 appearances and scoring 23 goals. He scored 17 goals in his final season there before moving to Ibrox, where he scored on his debut whilst the Gers toured America.

ANDY HALLIDAY

Andy grew up just metres away from Ibrox and the midfielder was a member of the Rangers Academy until he was 15 years old. He then moved to Livingston, where he started his senior career and made over 30 appearances for the Lions. The youngster then saw himself snapped up by Gordon Strachan at English Championship club Middlesbrough and he spent four years on Teesside. During his time with 'Boro, Halliday was loaned out to other English clubs, including Blackpool, where he was managed by former Rangers captain Barry Ferguson, and Walsall.

But it was Bradford who provided the next big step in his young career when he signed for the League One side permanently in the October of the 2014/15 season. Halliday was instrumental in Bradford's historic 4-2 FA Cup win over Chelsea – he scored the third goal in a game that has been dubbed one of the biggest cup shocks of all time.

Eight years after he left Rangers as a teenager Andy made his competitive first-team debut against Hibs in the Petrofac Cup and scored his first goal for the club on the same afternoon.

HARRY FORRESTER

Harry came through the youth ranks at Watford and Aston Villa, and while he made no senior appearances for either, he gained some experience of what to expect in Scottish football with a loan spell at Kilmarnock in season 2010/11. He made a total of eight appearances for Killie, the final of those coming as a substitute in a 3-2 defeat for the Ayrshire side to Walter Smith's Rangers in November 2010. From Villa, he spent time on trial with Ajax before joining Brentford in the summer of 2011 on a two-year deal, where he went on to make 69 appearances in all competitions and scored 11 goals in the process.

When his contract with the London club expired, Harry switched to Championship side Doncaster Rovers where he made 66 appearances and again scored 11 goals before making the switch to Rangers.

JOE DODOO

The attacker arrived from English Premier League champions Leicester City on a four-year deal.

The winger, who can also play as a central striker, had been training with the Light Blues before securing a deal having made his breakthrough into Claudio Ranieri's remarkable Leicester squad in the first half of last season.

He netted a hat-trick on his debut against Bury in the Capital One Cup, and followed that up with a goal against West Ham in the same competition, meaning overall he boasts a record of four goals in the four matches he played for the Foxes' first team.

Eligible to play for both Ghana and England, Dodoo has represented the Three Lions at youth level previously.

MATT CROOKS

The midfielder began his career as a youth at Manchester United before making the switch to Yorkshire and Huddersfield Town. In over three years there, he made just the one appearance before moving back across the counties to Lancashire and Accrington in November 2014.

For Stanley, he appeared 53 times and scored eight times from holding midfield, and contributed to them making the League Two play-offs at the end of the 2015/16 campaign.

Flexible in position like most of Mark Warburton's players, Crooks can also play in defence.

JOEY BARTON

One of the most recognisable figures in British football, Barton's signing was a real coup for Rangers.

He won the English Championship with Burnley last season and was named in the league's team of the year.

He has vast experience having played for a number of top clubs, including Premier League spells with Manchester City, Newcastle United and QPR. Barton has also had a spell in France's top league with Marseille and has been capped by the England national side.

In his trophy cabinet, he has two Championship winners' medals from Newcastle and Burnley, a play-off winners' medal from QPR, his Championship 'Team of the Year' gong and Burnley's Player of the Year award from last season.

TOM'S TOP TEN

Tom Miller has been a broadcaster and match commentator in the Scottish game for a host of major radio stations and TV channels.

He covered the first-ever game broadcast on the internet in Scotland in 1999 when Sunderland came to Ibrox for Ian Ferguson's testimonial and has been with RangersTV ever since.

A Rangers fan since the halcyon days of the early '60s, here are ten of Tom's top players to have worn the famous jersey.

> " I HAVE PICKED SOME FANTASTIC RANGERS PLAYERS OVER A NUMBER OF ERAS AND I HOPE THEY BRING BACK SOME GREAT MEMORIES FOR YOU.
>
> THEY CERTAINLY DO FOR ME! "

JOHN GREIG

He has the title of the greatest ever Ranger and his statue stands proudly at the corner of the Main and Copland Road stands at Ibrox. John is a Rangers icon having served the club as manager and also as a director after a 17-year distinguished one-club playing career. In today's transfer market John would be priceless.

A genuine leader of men who had a winning mentality as confirmed by a medal haul that includes five League titles, five League Cup successes and six times winner of the Scottish Cup. Three domestic Trebles were secured along the way and he also represented Scotland on 44 occasions.

John captained the side in Barcelona when the European Cup Winners' Cup was won and he remains a fantastic ambassador for the football club. John was one of my first footballing heroes and I remember as a youngster in the 1960s running alongside him to get his autograph after a game against Airdrie. He signed my book then jumped into his white Jaguar. I was star struck!

If you tried to find a modern player to compare to John Greig, take the tackling of Patrick Vieira, the energy of Wayne Rooney and the passing of Xavi of Barcelona and you will be on the right lines.

"SLIM" JIM BAXTER

Quite simply Baxter could make the ball talk. Another star of a phenomenally successful Rangers side of the early '60s that dominated Scottish football.

Baxter played with a swagger and had self-belief that set him apart.

His record against old rivals Celtic is quite remarkable having lost only twice against them in 18 match-ups.

Few would argue that Baxter was the most gifted footballer ever to wear the famous light blue shirt.

In the colours of Scotland, Baxter also excelled. Against England at Wembley in 1963, Scotland played most of the game with only 10 men after Eric Caldow, also of Rangers, had suffered a broken leg. It was long before the days of substitutes but Baxter took centre stage and scored both goals in Scotland's 2-1 win.

Four years later back at Wembley, Scotland became the first team to beat England after they had won the World Cup and it was Slim Jim who was tormentor-in-chief to the English superstars. Jim even had the confidence to play keepie uppie to further humiliate his opponents as Scotland won much more comfortably than the 3-2 score line suggests.

I was very lucky to be able to write his biography "Slim Jim – Simply the Best" and the title of the book says it all.

DAVID WEIR

Younger readers will know that David Weir is now Assistant Manager to Mark Warburton but as a player David only came to Rangers very late in his career. But what an impact he had during another wonderful period for the club.

Walter Smith had returned to replace Paul Le Guen and the first thing he did was offer 36-year-old David a short-term contract. He ended up staying five years and winning the Premier League three times!

David was the Scottish Premier League Player of the Year in 2010 and won the Scottish Football Writers' Player of the Year in the same season. David also captained the side to the UEFA Cup Final of 2008 in a season that saw him play an incredible 66 games.

While with Hearts, David had often been linked with a move to his boyhood heroes at Ibrox but he was transferred to Everton in 1999 instead.

With 69 caps for his country, David is Scotland's 6th most capped player and having him back as Assistant Manager means the traditions and values of the club will be maintained and new players will be fully aware of what's expected of them under David Weir, who is another member of Rangers' exclusive Hall of Fame.

MARTYN WAGHORN

When Mark Warburton signed Martyn for Rangers on the same day as his Wigan team-mate James Tavernier, not many fans knew much about the striker who had started his career at Sunderland where, as a 17-year-old, he had made his debut against Manchester United.

But the Rangers faithful didn't have long to wait to realise they had a new hero to worship. With a two-goal debut in the 6-2 demolition of Hibs everyone realised Waghorn had something special about him. Strong and athletic with a superb first touch and the wonderful poise and balance of a naturally gifted left-sided player, he claimed 28 goals in his first season as a Ranger.

Had it not been for injury against Kilmarnock in the Scottish Cup in early February, you have to think that tally would have been nearer 35 or more had he not missed such a big chunk of the season.

Martyn is clearly benefiting from having some stability in his career after loan spells at Hull and Millwall while with Leicester before joining Wigan for one season.

Martyn has a settled family life in Glasgow and Rangers are reaping the rewards. There are many more goals to come from Waggy, that's for sure!

STEVEN DAVIS

Steven Davis is a real players' player. He had an excellent European Championship campaign with Northern Ireland in the summer in France.

The boy from Ballymena nearly joined Rangers as a teenager but with no contract offer on the table he signed for Aston Villa.

After three years at Villa he moved to Fulham as he had caught the eye of Ewan Chester who had been Rangers Chief Scout until 2004 and was now in the same role at Craven Cottage.

When Walter Smith came back to manage Rangers in 2007, Ewan joined the club again as part of his backroom team.

It didn't take much for Ewan to encourage Walter to make Steven a Ranger. The Light Blues were in the market for an energetic box-to-box midfielder and Steven fitted the profile to a tee!

He originally came to Ibrox on loan but the deal was soon made permanent and Steven became a key player in the Rangers engine room.

Sadly the financial problems at Rangers in 2012 saw him move to Southampton but unlike a number of players who left around that time, Rangers received at least part of his true value as compensation.

In his time at Rangers Steven played 210 games for the club and scored 22 goals.

I wouldn't rule out him going on to win 100 caps for his country.

LEE WALLACE

Lee stayed for the journey. He is a model professional who now captains Rangers with pride.

Lee joined Rangers from Hearts in July 2011 after the clubs finally agreed a fee. It was money well spent by Ally McCoist who was then Rangers manager and Lee adapted to life on the other side of the M8 immediately.

Lee could easily become the only player in Scotland to win every division in the Scottish leagues as Rangers go for title number 55.

The defender made his Hearts debut in 2005 and made his first start for Scotland against Japan in 2009. He was in the international wilderness as Rangers fought their way back to the top of the Scottish game but will surely be consistently back in the dark blue of Scotland given his performances.

In the Championship-winning season of 2015/16, Lee added goals to his game, claiming 9 in the campaign and as a captain he has the total respect of the dressing-room and the fans alike.

Lee looks set to be a Ranger for life and he conducts himself on and off the park in the traditional style of other Rangers captains of the past.

A legend in the making.

WILLIE JOHNSTON

Willie Johnston remains the fastest player I have ever seen in a Rangers jersey. Willie was a real talent who loved to play to the crowd whether he was on the wing, an old-fashioned inside forward or a striker. His pace terrorised defenders.

Willie had two spells at Rangers but broke into the first team in 1964 and was playing for Scotland by the time he was 18.

Nicknamed 'Bud', he was a clear favourite of the fans even before he scored two goals in the European Cup-Winners' Cup Final in Barcelona as Rangers beat Dynamo Moscow 3-2 in what remains the finest hour for the club.

However, his performance in the semi-final at Ibrox is worth remembering, too. Goals from Sandy Jardine and Derek Parlane saw Rangers book their place in the final with a 2-0 win over Bayern Munich but Johnston had tormented the German defence from the first whistle.

At one point he raced at Bayern's international full-back Paul Breitner then stopped immediately in front of him and promptly sat on the ball with the game still going on. With a huge smile, Bud invited Breitner to come and take the ball but as soon as the defender came forward Bud was up and accelerated away from him! The home crowd loved it!

Controversy and Willie Johnston were never far apart including his well-documented banned substance use at the World Cup of 1978 but what a player. 393 appearances for the club and 125 goals.

ALISTAIR MCCOIST

With 355 goals for the club, Ally McCoist remains Rangers' all-time leading goal scorer.

His nickname from the fans, "Super Ally", says it all. Even former captain Lee McCulloch has McCoist's name in his phone as just `SUPER'.

As manager of the club, undoubtedly Ally had problems like none of his predecessors ever faced as he led the club through the turmoil and chaos from 2012. However, as a player with Rangers his success was phenomenal.

He is one of a very elite few that played in every season of the nine-in-a row era, yet when he first arrived from Sunderland in 1983 the fans were not convinced that manager John Greig had made a good choice as goals in those early days proved hard to come by.

But McCoist was of strong character and even when he fell out of favour in the tenure of Graeme Souness, he battled for his place in the team and never let his head go down. Twice winner of the European Golden Shoe award in 1992 and 1993, McCoist was well decorated throughout his career and has 10 League winner's medals in Scotland, nine League Cup successes but strangely only ever won the Scottish Cup on one occasion.

A true Ranger, Ally also represented Scotland 61 times and scored 19 goals, captaining his country once in 1996 against Australia and he even managed to score the only goal of that game. Super Ally indeed !

NACHO NOVO

Nacho was another fans' favourite and a natural goal scorer.

Converting the pressure penalty against Fiorentina in the UEFA Cup semi-final shoot out will ensure he will always have a place in Rangers' history.

Nacho joined Rangers in 2004 after rejecting the chance to sign for Celtic and was given the iconic squad No. 10 that had been vacated by Michael Mols and he didn't let anybody down. Nacho had arrived in Scotland three years before, joining Raith Rovers before moving on to Dundee. While with Huesca in the Spanish second division Nacho's agent had sent a video recording to my friend Peter Hetherston who was assistant manager at Stark's Park at the time and he couldn't wait to show me the `wee Spanish guy' he was going to sign.

So I actually saw Nacho before almost everyone else in Scotland. Yes he was raw but he was lightning quick and only wanted to score goals. Score he did for Raith and Dundee before he got his big move to Rangers.

Nacho scored 73 career goals for the Light Blues, with his best season being his second at the club when he netted 25 times.

He was often used as the modern day impact player, coming off the bench because of his ability to change games, and this was never more evident than in the 2009 Scottish Cup Final against Falkirk when the teams were tied at 0-0. 28 seconds after Nacho's introduction he scored and Rangers took the trophy.

Nacho became the first Spaniard to be honoured with a place in Rangers' Hall of Fame when he was inducted in 2014.

BRIAN LAUDRUP & PAUL GASCOIGNE

Some things are just meant to be paired together. Mince and tatties, fish and chips and Gazza and Laudrup.

What a dynamic pair they were together in a rampant Rangers side in the mid to late 1990s. They were kings of the Scottish game as the Light Blues swept aside all challengers for domestic honours.

Brian Laudrup arrived first in the summer of 1994 from Fiorentina for a fee of £2.3 million and Gazza also came from Italian football, leaving Lazio for Ibrox one year later.

After only a few months at Ibrox, Laudrup was a target for Barcelona but he turned them down saying he was enjoying his football and life in Glasgow.

It's fair to say, too, that Paul Gascoigne had the best spell of his career while with Rangers and he also settled well into life in Scotland.

Many will say that Laudrup's finest hour came in the Scottish Cup Final of 1996 when he scored two and set up a hat-trick for striker Gordon Durie as Hearts were broken 5-1.

When the great Dane signed, Ally McCoist was quoted as saying: "Instructions were simple – give Brian the ball then get out his road when he got it!"

Gascgoine's signing set a new transfer record for the club when they paid £4.3 million for his services.

His impact was immediate, delivering a wonder goal in his first Old Firm game when he ran the length of the field from deep inside his own half to score.

In 1996 Paul scored a stunning hat trick as Aberdeen were beaten on the second last day of the season and eight-in-a row was secured. The following season the title was won again and Gazza was a major influence in the side, scoring 17 goals from midfield.

A complex character but a genius sums Gazza up. He had his demons but as a player with Rangers he was a joy to watch.

WORD SEARCH

Can you find 10 Rangers in our Wordsearch?
You can go horizontally, vertically, diagonally, and backwards.

```
C K B G M N N A C C M
Q C P A O K X N F W M
G T R E E U M L O R N
Y O F Q N X G O H V O
G K Y M G I D H N K S
Y T J O I S D I F B R
L L Y O O H E R G K E
K M P R C T Q L A D H
P R T E S M M T V J P
N P K P A R L A N E C
R N R R G N K W Q L M
```

| Gascoigne | Gough | McCann | Moore | Stein |
| Goram | Jardine | McPherson | Parlane | Woods |

Answers on page 60/61.

NEW SIGNINGS

JOE GARNER

Striker Joe Garner arrived at Ibrox from Preston North End on a three-year deal in August.

The 28 year-old, who made his first-team debut at Kilmarnock that same month, has a wealth of experience at both English Championship and League One level having played his part in the Lillywhites, securing 11th place in England's second tier in their first season back at that level with six goals.

That they made it to the Championship at all was largely down to Garner as he hit a total of 27 goals in season 2014/15 where Preston eventually made it up through the play-offs with victory over Wes Foderingham's Swindon Town.

His career began as a youth player at hometown club Blackburn Rovers before being loaned to and then signed by Carlisle United.

A record of 14 goals in 31 appearances in his one season in Cumbria saw him earn a £1.1million move to Nottingham Forest in 2008 where he scored 10 goals in 55 appearances over three seasons, although his final season in the Midlands saw him loaned to both Huddersfield and Scunthorpe.

Watford was next up for Garner, with his two-year spell there including another loan period at Carlisle before Preston snapped him up in January 2013, where in all, he hit 57 goals.

PHILIPPE SENDEROS

Defender Philippe Senderos was Mark Warburton's final signing of the summer transfer window.

The former Arsenal star penned a one-year deal after a successful trial period and brought with him vast experience having performed at a top level throughout Europe.

The Switzerland international has appeared at three World Cups and a European Championships, with over 50 international caps to his credit.

He began his career at Swiss Super League outfit Servette before making the move to the Gunners in 2003. While not appearing in the 'Invincibles' team of the 2004/05 season, he made his breakthrough the following campaign and played in the 2006 FA Cup Final where Arsenal defeated Manchester United on penalties in Cardiff.

In all, he spent seven seasons in North London, and featured on the bench in the 2006 Champions League final in Paris where Arsene Wenger's side lost 2-1 to Barcelona.

Loan spells at AC Milan and Everton followed in 2008 and 2009 respectively before he moved permanently to Fulham in 2010, staying at Craven Cottage for four seasons. La Liga's Valencia were next up for Senderos, spending one season there in 2013-14 before heading back to England and Aston Villa. His last club was Grasshoppers in Zurich.

THANK YOU EVERYONE!

Founders Trail delighted with progress over past few years.

We would like to share with you, the Rangers Family, a message from the Founders Trail as they discuss the ongoing productive relationship that they have built with the club over the years.

"Since the first Founders Trail seven years ago we have gradually built a close relationship with Rangers Football Club.

"Working with the club has been a huge part of our success.

"The current Board of Directors recognises the importance of celebrating the history of our great club and they are keen to help promote the incredible story of the four boys who formed Rangers and the others who nurtured it. We are thankful for their support.

"In turn, we want to continue to celebrate our history and to promote the club in any way we can.

"The Founders Trail is completely self-funding.

"The bus hire, the literature you receive when you take the tour and the continued research is only possible because of the incredible backing we have received from you, the Rangers support.

"The demand for the tours is continuing to grow and we thank you for letting us share the history of Rangers with you.

"When you purchase a seat on the Founders Trail bus, you

not only give us the opportunity to tell the Rangers story, you also help to put funds back into the club. Your money goes towards the purchase of:

- **Match day tickets** (used as raffle prizes)
- **Argyle House Restaurant vouchers** (used as raffle prizes)
- **Ibrox Stadium Tours**
- **Rangers Lottery**
- **Youth Members Club**
- **Auchenhowie Brick**
- **Donations to the Rangers Youth Development Company**

"The Founders Trail and Ibrox Stadium Tour is very proud to run in association with Rangers Football Club and Rangers Youth Development Company.

"We include adverts for the Rangers Youth Development Company in our tour literature to help highlight the ways the fans can contribute to the success of our youth teams.

"The close working relationship we have with the Club has also allowed us to begin using the Parks of Hamilton coaches for the tours.

"Argyle House Restaurant kindly lets us offer our passengers a 10% discount on any meal.

"And the media team at Rangers are very keen to help spread the word of our Founders.

"They have highlighted tour dates and published blogs from the Founders Trail team on the official club website, as well as on other social media platforms.

"We hope this productive relationship continues to grow in the years to come."

For more information, please email:
thegallantpioneers@googlemail.com.

Jordan jumped at chance to join

CLUB'S RICH HISTORY MADE DECISION TO MOVE SO SIMPLE

Players have been known to do homework to learn information on their new club but for Jordan Rossiter, no history lesson was required when he swapped Liverpool for Rangers.

Having been among the legions of Light Blues fans who descended on the City of Manchester Stadium in 2008 to watch the UEFA Cup Final, the 19-year-old was well versed in all things Rangers prior to his summer switch.

Eight years after his Euro adventure as a young boy, the teenager didn't have to think twice before leaving behind the fabled Anfield for the hallowed turf of Ibrox.

"It is a great club with a lot of history," said the midfielder, who signed a four-year deal having been out of contract at Liverpool.

"I have come from a massive club like Liverpool to another massive club like Rangers so it is a great feeling for me and an honour.

"I know Frank McParland (Head of Recruitment) from my Liverpool days and working with the academy with him and he is a great fella.

"He didn't need to sell the club to me, it doesn't need much selling. You look at Murray Park, which is a great training facility and then Ibrox; I walked into Ibrox and I was a bit taken aback by it.

"I walked in and saw all the mahogany walls and it's nice and old, you can tell it is a stadium with a lot of history and I'm sure there will be a lot more made there in the future.

"I chose Rangers because of the history it has got, it is a massive club and I don't think people realise down south how big a club it really is.

"I went to the final down in Manchester a few years ago which was unbelievable. Someone had a spare ticket and Liverpool only being 45 minutes from Manchester I went along and the fans were brilliant that day.

"Going to that game and seeing them on telly I have seen what a brilliant set of fans they are.

"I think I have always known what a big club Rangers is and so have my family, and it is just a great opportunity to carry on learning my trade.

"They have been in the Champions League and UEFA Cup Finals, it is a club with a great tradition in Europe and I am sure I can bring something to that."

Jordan made his debut for his new club as a second-half substitute in the League Cup victory over Stranraer at Ibrox in July, ending something of a waiting game for the talented youngster with the contract having been penned two months earlier.

International duty with the England Under 19s at the European Championships in Germany meant his arrival north was delayed a little.

But after making his bow in front of the Ibrox faithful, he said: "It was some feeling. I signed back in May and waited a long time to make my debut being away with England at the Euros.

"It was a great reception, the fans here are brilliant. I knew that because everyone always talks about Rangers fans and that they are one of the best in the world so I really enjoyed it.

"The atmosphere was unbelievable, it's probably one of the biggest crowds that I've played in front of. It was really good to get on and get your first few touches of the ball so you can work your way into the game and I loved every minute of it.

"The lads are great, with lots of experienced lads and younger lads too, they're a good group of lads in the changing room and they've helped me to fit in well. All of the lads have been brilliant at helping me to settle in.

"It's a great city, everyone is really friendly and I'm looking forward to staying here."

BACK where he belongs

Danny Wilson has no regrets about returning for second spell at Ibrox.

Danny Wilson is delighted to be back where it all started.

The cultured defender returned to Ibrox in the summer if 2015, five years after his dream move to Liverpool and he's loving life just as much second time around.

The centre-half retraced his steps to Govan after captaining Hearts to Championship success but while many observers doubted the wisdom of turning his back on the top flight, the Light Blues star was convinced he was making the right choice.

With another Championship medal in his collection and Rangers back in the Premiership, Danny has no regrets.

"There was some doubt surrounding the club after the season it had just had and a lot of people were saying I shouldn't have signed again and instead gone elsewhere," he said.

"I had just captained Hearts to the Championship and won promotion to the top flight but I just felt in the interests of long-term success, Rangers was a better option. It is a big club and I thought I would have more opportunities to be successful here and I have no doubts in my mind that will be the case going forward.

"For me it was always the right decision. I had nothing but good memories from my time before at the club and when I spoke to the management team, it felt the only decision I could make as they made me feel wanted.

"I understood the way they wanted the team to play, they saw me as a big part of that and I was delighted to be able to get something done.

"To be honest it was a bit strange when I came in to speak to the management as there were a lot of familiar faces still here behind the scenes. I was getting hugs from the canteen ladies and security folk and it was a nice feeling. It was a bit strange but familiar at the same time as I had been at the place since I was eight until 18.

"In many ways I felt I was back at a place I was meant to be."

His return journey has taken Danny via Anfield and Tynecastle, and he believes Rangers are reaping the benefits of his time away.

"When I left Ibrox, it was for various reasons," he said. "I was maybe a wee bit young but feel now the different experiences I have had have made me a better player and a better person.

"Although I left, I always thought I'd like to come back one day. It has happened a bit sooner than I maybe thought but I'm delighted the way things have worked out.

"To be a part of taking Rangers back to the Premiership, the top tier of Scottish football where we belong, was a big factor for me. The chance to be part of that history was a big pull and I'm just very happy to be back and enjoying my football and enjoying my life off the pitch as well."

Having been captain of Hearts, Danny knows what it takes to shoulder such a responsibility and he's been hugely impressed by the manner in which Lee Wallace has assumed the skipper's role at Ibrox.

Handed the armband by Mark Warburton, the left-back has responded in magnificent fashion, as his team-mate acknowledged.

"I'm not the captain here but I know how important it is to have other players around you who can help," said Danny.

"When I was at Hearts, more so in my second season as captain, I had seasoned professionals who were my sounding boards I could go to if I had a problem or if I needed a bit of help.

"I know how important that is for Lee. He has players he can come to and I'm always happy to give him my input if he needs it. I can see what a great job Lee is doing as captain on and off the field and how worthy he is of the captaincy.

"He is a great leader. I know how difficult it can be as captain and credit to him for the job he is doing."

GUESS WHO?

We've mixed up a few Rangers head shots to make some weird and wonderful faces. Can you work out whose hair, eyes and chins are pictured?

Answers on p60/61.

HAIR:

EYES:

CHIN:

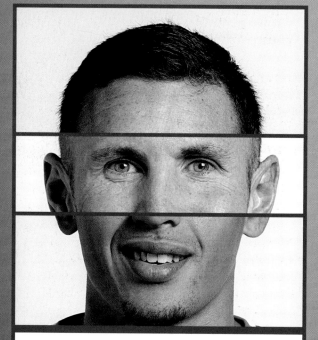

HAIR:

EYES:

CHIN:

HAIR:

EYES:

CHIN:

CROSSWORD

ACROSS

1 He scored Rangers' first goal in the 2016/17 Betfred League Cup group stage. (9)

4 Liverpool Academy Player of the Year, Season 2013/14. (8)

6 Goalkeeper Matt Gilks previously played for this 'seaside' team. (9)

11 Clint Hill began his career at this club. (8)

13 The father of Josh Windass played for this Scottish club. (8)

14 He has represented Scotland at under-19, under-20 and under-21 level. (4)

16 Club captain since Mark Warburton arrived as manager. (7)

18 Andy Halliday scored here on a memorable FA Cup victory for Bradford in Season 2014/15. (8,6)

19 He opened the scoring against Celtic in the semi-final of the Scottish Cup, April 2016. (6)

20 Nine-in-a-row was secured at this venue. (9)

DOWN

2 Rangers' points tally for the 2015/16 Scottish Championship campaign. (6,3)

3 Born in Livingston, West Lothian. (6)

5 Season 2008/09, he was captain of Watford's under-18 side. (7)

7 Rangers' first foreign manager. (8)

8 Niko Kranjcar has over 80 caps for this country. (7)

9 Martyn Waghorn's squad number for the 2016/17 campaign. (6,5)

10 Joey Barton arrived at Ibrox after helping which side achieve promotion to the English Premiership? (7)

12 The first player to be inducted into the Hall of Fame whilst under contract at Rangers. (4)

15 Barrie McKay began his career as a youth player with this Scottish Premiership side. (10)

17 This manager won more trophies than any other manager in the history of Scottish football. (6)

Cup of Cheer

Rampant Rangers completed a successful Petrofac Training Cup campaign with a comprehensive victory over Peterhead at Hampden Park.

Here we take a look back at the run to the final, where the Blue Toon was put to the sword in some style.

Speaking after the cup triumph, manager Mark Warburton said: "I'm delighted for the supporters. The level of support we had was magnificent."

Saturday, July 25, 2015

HIBS 2, RANGERS 6

Scorers: Tavernier, Waghorn (2), Halliday, Miller (2)

Mark Warburton's first competitive match in charge could not have gone better with Rangers recording a quite stunning victory over Hibs at Easter Road.

The Edinburgh outfit had no answer to a rampant Gers side but it had looked so different when Sam Stanton had given the hosts the lead after 15 minutes.

The advantage wasn't to last long, however, with new signings James Tavernier and Martyn Waghorn launching their Ibrox careers in style with a goal apiece before the interval.

Waghorn grabbed his second of a pulsating match shortly after the restart before Jason Cummings pulled one back. Any thoughts of a recovery, however, were snuffed out when another debutant, Andy Halliday, netted before Kenny Miller blasted a quick-fire double against his former club.

RANGERS: Foderingham, Tavernier, Kiernan, Wilson, Wallace, Holt (Shiels 60), Halliday, Law, McKay, Waghorn (Clark 74), Templeton (Miller 60). Subs not used: Kelly, McGregor, Aird, Thompson.

Wednesday, August 19, 2015

AYR UNITED 0, RANGERS 2

Scorers: Clark, McKay

Rangers continued their cup campaign with a solid performance at a windswept Somerset Park.

The driving rain added to the difficult conditions but goals in either half from Nicky Clark and Barrie McKay secured a safe passage through to the next round.

It was a pleasing clean sheet for the Ibrox side, something which would become a recurring theme throughout the remainder of the tournament.

RANGERS: Foderingham, Tavernier (Aird 81), Ball, Wilson, Wallace, Shiels, Holt, Walsh (Law 59), Oduwa, McKay (Waghorn 72), Clark. Subs not used: Kelly, Kiernan, Miller, Halliday.

Tuesday, October 20, 2015

RANGERS 1, LIVINGSTON 0

Scorer: Clark

The hosts left it late to overcome Livingston, Nicky Clark netting the only goal of the game against the holders.

When it arrived, 15 minutes from time, it was an effort worthy of winning any game, the 25-yard drive giving the Lions keeper no chance.

The visitors from West Lothian had frustrated Rangers for long spells but it was the Light Blues who progressed to the semi-finals and a clash against St Mirren.

RANGERS: Foderingham, Tavernier, Ball, Kiernan, Wallace, Halliday, Holt, Law, McKay, Waghorn, Oduwa (Clark 45). Subs not used: Kelly, Walsh, Hardie, Thompson, Aird, Miller.

Saturday, November 28, 2015

RANGERS 4, ST MIRREN 0
Scorers: Holt, Miller, Waghorn, Kelly (og)

Rangers made no mistake in the semi-final as they swept aside St Mirren at Ibrox Stadium. The teams went in at the break on level terms but a powerful second-half display booked the home side's ticket to Hampden Park in April.

Jason Holt broke the deadlock and goals from Martyn Waghorn and Kenny Miller made the game safe before an own goal from Sean Kelly in the closing minutes.

RANGERS:
Foderingham, Tavernier, Kiernan, Wilson, Wallace, Halliday, Holt (Shiels 63), Zelalem, Waghorn, Miller (Hardie 7), McKay (Clark 63). Subs not used: Kelly, Ball, Aird, Oduwa.

Sunday, April 10, 2016

RANGERS 4, PETERHEAD 0
Scorers: Gilchrist (og), Tavernier, Halliday, Miller

All roads led to Hampden Park as Rangers took on Peterhead in the final of the Petrofac Cup and the team didn't disappoint by producing an impressive display to sweep aside the challenge of the League One side.

The Light Blues were sent on their way by an own goal from Ally Gilchrist before further strikes from James Tavernier, Andy Halliday and Kenny Miller completed the comfortable win.

Petrofac Training Cup Final

WINNERS 2016

The final whistle was met by roars of delight by the legions of Light Blues fans in the crowd of over 48,000 as they hailed the first trophy won by manager Mark Warburton .

RANGERS: Foderingham, Tavernier, Kiernan, Wilson, Wallace (O'Halloran 65), Ball, Halliday, Holt, Forrester (King 65), Miller, McKay (Shiels 78). Subs not used: Bell, Law, Clark, Zelalem.

RANGERS CHARITY FOUNDATION

As well as being passionate about football, Rangers is also passionate about what the club stands for off the pitch.

The Rangers Charity Foundation embodies the strong charitable values of the Rangers Family and a spirit that everyone connected with the club can feel proud of.

The Foundation works with charity partners each season to fund projects that have a lasting and significant impact in our community and beyond. Most recently, the club has worked with Glasgow City Mission's Winter Night Shelter, Alzheimer Scotland, the Glasgow Children's Hospital Charity, four services-related charities and Unicef, the world's leading children's charity. This season the Foundation looks forward to continuing the relationship with a number of these special charities as well as working with some exciting new organisations.

The Foundation is also very proud of its work in the community. Every season it helps thousands of fundraisers support causes close to their hearts by making in-kind donations and assisting various community initiatives such as the local food bank.

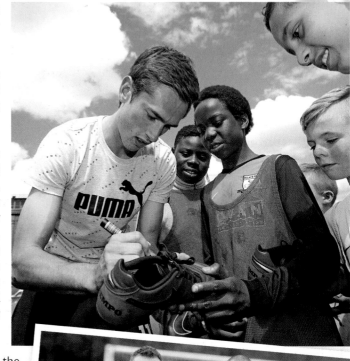

The comprehensive community programme also reaches thousands of children and adults with important messages and workshops regarding health and wellbeing, employability and education. The community programmes support many local people, including veterans, people who are recovering from addictions and Rangers fans who are trying to lose weight. The Foundation also works with a number of local schools delivering key equality, health and wellbeing messages.

The Foundation organises Rangers 'Dream Days' twice a season, inviting children and adults who have been through an illness or tough time to visit the club's world-class training centre at Murray Park, meet the entire first team squad, watch the team train and enjoy an exclusive tour of the facility before travelling to Ibrox for lunch and a tour of the stadium.

Across the country, thousands of people every week set out to raise money for a charitable cause close to their heart and the Foundation is there to help whenever it can. It makes in-kind donations to charities, community groups and other worthwhile causes worth thousands of pounds every year.

The Foundation also arranges hospital visits by the players from time to time when fans are too ill to travel and tries to respond to as many deserving cases as possible, brightening the lives of children and adults who are battling a serious medical condition or disability.

The Foundation organises a number of fantastic events of its own throughout the season that everyone can get involved in, from a Charity Ball to a True Blue Hero Fun Run and even Big Ibrox Sleep Outs in the stadium – there is something for everyone. Every single person who takes part in an event for us also has the chance to become a True Blue Hero, where you will be invited along to a special reception at Ibrox and be presented with a medal by a first team player. If you can't take part in any organised events why not take on your own personal challenge? As long as you raise over £100 you will become a True Blue Hero!

The Foundation also helps by providing charities with the opportunity to hold a can collection at Ibrox Stadium, donating complimentary

match tickets to community groups and sending letters and goodie bags to children and adults in hospital.

To date, over £4.2 million in cash and in-kind support has been donated – something everyone connected with the Foundation can all be very proud of!

Find out more about the Rangers Charity Foundation's work and all the latest news by visiting www.rangerscharity.org.uk or contact the Foundation team on 0141 580 8775 or by emailing rangerscharity@rangers.co.uk.

FORM IN THE USA

THURSDAY, JULY 7, 2016

CHARLESTON BATTERY 1, RANGERS 2

SCORERS: Windass, Forrester

RANGERS: Foderingham (Gilks 45), Tavernier (Ross McCrorie 69), Onyewu (Wilson 45), Wilson (Hill 12 (Onyewu 69)), Wallace (Walsh 60), Halliday, Holt (Forrester 60), Windass (Hardie 60), Waghorn (Thompson 60), Miller (O'Halloran 45), Walsh (McKay 45).

It was destination USA as Rangers put the finishing touches to their pre-season preparations in the summer.

The Light Blues crossed the Atlantic to steamy South Carolina, where they enjoyed a 10-day training camp to help prepare for their return to the Premiership.

Charleston Battery provided the opposition in the only game played by Rangers during the trip, with second-half goals from Josh Windass and Harry Forrester enough to secure victory.

Boss Mark Warburton utilised all his available outfield players in the game which provided an important workout in the heat of Charleston, though the action was delayed by over an hour due to an electrical storm.

FIRM FAVOURITES

Rangers' welcome ascent to the Scottish Premiership after four years has seen the return of the Old Firm league fixture to the SPFL calendar.

The meeting with Celtic is a clash which has grabbed the interest of football fans throughout the world ever since the two teams first locked horns.

Here we look back on a handful of stirring Rangers triumphs, in both league and cup competitions.

SATURDAY, MAY 5, 1973
SCOTTISH CUP FINAL
RANGERS 3, CELTIC 2
SCORERS: PARLANE, CONN JNR, FORSYTH

The incredible Centenary Cup Final attracted a crowd of 122,000 at Hampden Park.

In an amazing match, Rangers edged a five-goal thriller with defender Tom Forsyth scoring the winning goal.

The Light Blues had gone into the game as underdogs with Celtic having won their eighth successive title but after the European Cup Winners' Cup triumph 12 months earlier, their performance served as a timely reminder that Rangers were setting the foundations to challenge their arch-rivals again.

RANGERS: McCloy, Jardine, Mathieson, Forsyth, Johnstone, Greig, MacDonald, Conn Jnr, McLean, Parlane, Young.

SUNDAY, MAY 2, 1999
PREMIER LEAGUE
CELTIC 0, RANGERS 3
SCORERS: MCCANN (2), ALBERTZ

There was plenty at stake as the teams kicked off with Rangers aware that a win would secure them the title at the home of their biggest rivals.

The stormy encounter saw Celtic reduced to nine men and referee Hugh Dallas struck on the head by a coin thrown from the crowd.

Two goals from Neil McCann and a penalty converted by Jorg Albertz helped Rangers to clinch the championship at Parkhead for the only time in their history, their 10th title in 11 years.

RANGERS: Klos, Porrini, Amoruso, Vidmar, Hendry, Van Bronckhorst, Albertz, McCann, Reyna, Wallace, Amato.

SUBS: Niemi, McInnes, Johansson, Wilson, Riccio.

SATURDAY, MAY 29, 1999
SCOTTISH CUP FINAL
CELTIC 0, RANGERS 1
SCORER: WALLACE

Rangers won the first Old Firm Scottish Cup final in 10 years, giving them a sixth domestic treble and denying Celtic a single trophy in a painful season for the Parkhead club.

The only goal of the game arrived in the second half, with Englishman Rod Wallace carving himself a little niche in the club's history.

A ball was played into the Celtic box, which Neil McCann managed to turn behind Wallace's man-marker Annoni.

Just six yards out with Gould to beat, the former Leeds United ace made no mistake to score his 27th goal of a productive first season in Scotland.

RANGERS: Klos, Porrini, Hendry, Amoruso, Vidmar, McCann, McInnes, Van Bronckhorst, Wallace, Amato, Albertz.

SUBS: Ferguson, Wilson, Kanchelskis.

SATURDAY, NOVEMBER 26, 2000
PREMIER LEAGUE
RANGERS 5, CELTIC 1
SCORERS: FERGUSON, FLO, DE BOER, MOLS, AMORUSO

This was a day to savour for the legions of faithful Rangers fans.

Inspired by Barry Ferguson, the Ibrox men racked up their greatest win against Celtic for 12 years on a day when they simply had to win and a jubilant home support could scarcely believe their eyes.

Ferguson led the charge with a captain's goal while £12million man Tore Andre Flo delivered the crucial second goal. Michael Mols and Ronald de Boer also netted their first Old Firm goals in their first taste of this fixture, while Lorenzo Amoruso got the other with a great header.

It was simply an unbelievable day as Rangers defied the critics and breathed new life into the title campaign.

RANGERS: Klos, Wilson, Konterman, Amoruso, Reyna, Ferguson, De Boer (Tugay 86), Albertz, Numan, Flo (McCann 86), Miller (Mols 60).

SUBS NOT USED: Christiansen, Ross.

SATURDAY, MAY 4, 2002
SCOTTISH CUP FINAL
RANGERS 3, CELTIC 2
SCORERS: LOVENKRANDS (2), FERGUSON

The Light Blues showed all their battling qualities to emerge victorious as a last-minute strike by Peter Lovenkrands gave Rangers the spoils in a stunning Scottish Cup Final.

Celtic had twice been ahead but Lovenkrands produced the first equaliser, Barry Ferguson the second before the Great Dane grabbed the winner.

The victory brought Rangers their 30th Scottish Cup title before 51,000 fans at Hampden Park.

It denied Celtic a league and cup double and gave Rangers their second piece of silverware, Alex McLeish having already lifted the CIS Insurance Cup.

RANGERS: Klos, Ross, Moore, Amoruso, Numan, Ricksen, de Boer, Ferguson, Lovenkrands, McCann, Caniggia (Arveladze 20).

SUBS NOT USED: McGregor, Vidmar, Nerlinger, Flo.

SUNDAY, APRIL 17, 2016
SCOTTISH CUP SEMI-FINAL
RANGERS 2, CELTIC 2 (AET)
SCORERS: MILLER, MCKAY
Rangers won 5-4 on penalties.

The hype surrounding last season's Scottish Cup semi-final showdown reached fever pitch as the big day approached – and it was Rangers who handled the huge occasion better than their old rivals.

The Ibrox side may have been underdogs but they reached the Scottish Cup Final in dramatic fashion as they defeated Celtic on penalties in a pulsating game.

In normal time Kenny Miller had opened the scoring on 16 minutes with a superbly taken goal as Mark Warburton's side dominated the opening exchanges. Celtic levelled through Erik Sviatchenko just after the break and the game went into extra time.

Barrie McKay scored arguably his most stunning goal in a blue jersey as he swung a superb 25-yard shot into the top corner six minutes into extra time. But, as they had done earlier, Celtic levelled after the break through Tomas Rogic and penalties beckoned.

Tense doesn't begin to describe the shoot-out but it was Rogic who missed the decisive 14th spot kick of the shoot-out and as it sailed over the bar it handed the Light Blues a superb 5-4 win.

RANGERS: Foderingham, Tavernier, Wilson, Kiernan (Zelalem 87), Wallace, Halliday, Ball, Shiels (Law 65), Holt, McKay, Miller (Clark 90).

SUBS NOT USED: Bell, Burt.

QUIZGERS

Test your **RANGERS** knowledge!

Answers on page 60/61.

1. In what year did Rangers win the European Cup Winners' Cup?

2. Where was the final played?

3. Against which team did Rangers clinch promotion to the Premiership?

4. What was the score?

5. How many times have Rangers been crowned Scottish League champions?

6. What do Danny Wilson and Jason Holt have in common?

7. Who did Rangers defeat in the final of the Petrofac Cup?

8. Can you name the scorers?

9. What is the all-seated capacity of Ibrox Stadium?

10. True or false: Former captain Richard Gough was born in South Africa.

11. How many league goals did Ally McCoist score for Rangers?

12. On what road is Ibrox Stadium located?

13. Martyn Waghorn signed from which club?

14. What was Joey Barton's last club before coming to Rangers?

15. Rangers played against what team in their first game back in the Premiership?

STADIUM TOURS

Get behind the scenes.

BOOK YOUR
STADIUM TOUR TODAY

rangers.co.uk | **0871 702 1972*** | **Rangers Ticket Centre**

*Calls cost 13p per minute plus network extras.

Quiz Answers

WORDSEARCH (PAGE 36)

C	K	B	G	M	N	N	A	C	C	M
Q	C	P	A	O	K	X	N	F	W	M
G	T	R	E	E	U	M	L	O	R	N
Y	O	F	Q	N	X	G	O	H	V	O
G	K	Y	M	G	I	D	H	N	K	S
Y	T	J	O	I	S	D	I	F	B	R
L	L	Y	O	O	H	E	R	G	K	E
K	M	P	R	C	T	Q	L	A	D	H
P	R	T	E	S	M	M	T	V	J	P
N	P	K	P	A	R	L	A	N	E	C
R	N	R	R	G	N	K	W	Q	L	M

QUIZGERS (PAGE 58)

1. 1972

2. Nou Camp, Barcelona

3. Dumbarton.

4. Rangers 1, Dumbarton 0

5. 54

6. Both players joined from Heart of Midlothian FC.

7. Peterhead

8. Gilchrist own goal, Tavernier, Halliday, Miller

9. 51,082

10. False. He was born in Sweden.

11. 251

12. Edmiston Drive

13. Wigan Athletic

14. Burnley

15. Hamilton Accies

CROSSWORD (PAGE 45)

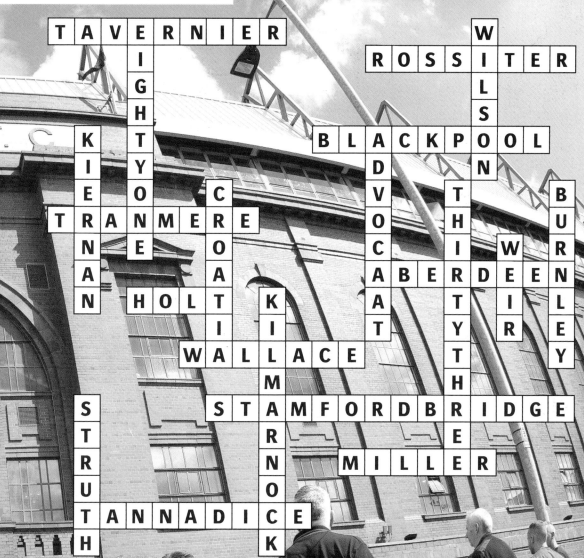

Across and down answers:

- TAVERNIER
- WILSON
- ROSSITER
- EIGHTYONE (vertical)
- KIERNAN
- BLACKPOOL
- TRANMERE
- ADVOCAAT (vertical)
- CREOATII / CROATIA (vertical)
- THIRTYTHREE (vertical)
- BURNLEY (vertical)
- HOLT
- KILMARNOCK (vertical)
- WEIR
- ABERDEEN
- WALLACE
- STRUTH (vertical)
- STAMFORD BRIDGE
- MILLER
- TANNADICE

WHO AM I? (PAGE 44)

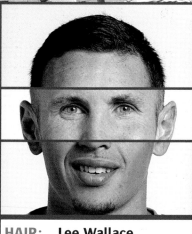

HAIR:	Lee Wallace
EYES:	Kenny Miller
CHIN:	James Tavernier

HAIR:	Barrie McKay
EYES:	Rob Kiernan
CHIN:	Danny Wilson

HAIR:	Wes Foderingham
EYES:	Andy Halliday
CHIN:	Martyn Waghorn